The Gnostic Hotel

Robert DiNapoli

THE GNOSTIC HOTEL
Robert DiNapoli

Published by Littlefox Press
PO Box 816
Kyneton VIC 3144

Copyright © 2021 Robert DiNapoli
ISBN 978-0-6480838-7-0

Cover artwork by Jon DiNapoli

No part of this book may be resold, hired out, reproduced, stored in a retrieval system or transmitted in any form or by any electronic, mechanical or other means without the prior written consent of the author or the publisher.

as ever,

for

Caz, Jon, Mim and Bec

Thanks and Acknowledgements

Heartfelt thanks to my closest readers,
Carolyn Masel, Christine Mathieu and Jill Morrow

and to everyone who has given the pieces in this book (and the thought behind them) attention, discussion and encouragement, especially

Chris Bishop, Kate Burridge, Diana Cousens,
Valerie Krips, Katie Mirabella, Sue Rechter
and Richard Wrigley

To work with Littlefox Press and its editor, Christine Mathieu, has been as great a pleasure as it is a privilege.

Special thanks to Jon DiNapoli for his eloquent cover artwork. More of his art and animation can be found at
https://jondinapoli.life

https://robertdinapoli.com
http://themelbourneliteratureseminars.com.au
bob.dinapoli@yahoo.com.au

The Vestibule

My study is a waiting room that bids
me pause, reflect and ponder at the door
of older minds than mine, whose ample lids
have opened onto vistas that my poor
imagination registers as hums,
scarce audible, from unseen surgeries,
where I am due to enter when time comes
and undergo procedural degrees
of metamorphic inside-out unpack,
a sifting of my whole life's manifest,
while my old hat and coat hang on the rack,
consigned, unlike the rest of me, to rest
until such time as we re-join the throng
of souls refreshed and opened to high song.

Contents

Introduction 1
Geworfenheit: The Gnostic Hotel 5
Agency 7
Psyops: y/n 8
Nomenclature: A Gnostic
Sleigh-Ride 9
Nella Selva Oscura: The Demiurge 10
The Gnostic Labyrinth 11

BY THE WATERS OF BABYLON
i. The Babylonian Exile 13
ii. Early Morning Departure
Lounge 14
iii. Emigré 15
iv. Building Babylon 15
v. The Makaris 16
vi. New Year's Day: Wisdom
in Exile 20

GNOSTIC LIFE IN WARTIME
i. *Realitätsprinzip* 22
ii. The Scholar Sentinel 22
iii. Trench Warfare 23
iv. *Das Boot* 24
vi. No Man's Land 24
vi. Earnest of Game 25

Gnostic Interrogatives 27
Debutante 28
Learning Curve 29
Signs of the Times 31
End-Times Etiquette 34
Taurus Minor in *Ellorhwær* 36
Kenosis: The Dirigible of Hermes
Trismegistus 37
The Divorce of Mind and Matter 39

40 The Errant Knight
41 Garden Lore
42 Your Study in the Bardo

ORPHEUS AND EURYDICE
43 i. Farewell
43 ii. Not at Home
44 iii. Scatterings
44 iv. Absence Resolves
45 v. The Retired Mountaineer
45 vi. The Chymical Assay

47 The Fishers of Fissures
48 The Magi's Visitation
49 The Etheric Twist
50 On the Threshold
51 Transcribal March
53 The Smuggler
54 Blowback
56 Signatures

ANTHROPOSOPHICAL PANDEMICAL ASSAYS
58 i. Into the Woods
58 ii. The Rock Ensouled
59 iii. Going Viral
59 iv. The Ascent
60 v. *Apocalypsis*
61 vi. Pneumatic Seismometer

62 *Requiescat*
63 The March Lands
64 Selfie de l'Isle

Introduction

The poems that follow pursue a long fascination with the thought-worlds of Gnosticism and Anthroposophy. The latter is recent, both the word itself and the psychospiritual orientation it names. The former is at least as old as Christianity. 'Anthroposophy' is the name given to a mode of 'occult science' by its founding figure, the German philosopher, lecturer and polymath Rudolf Steiner (1861-1925). Its bearings are both wide-ranging and subtle. Many of its principles and practices calmly offend modern habits of thought and have attracted both dedicated followers and equally determined sceptics and debunkers. In the broadest terms, it understands the human as a primarily psychic phenomenon, a gradual process of incarnation, across multiple lifetimes, through which our pre-existent spirit-selves immerse themselves ever more deeply into the world of matter, space and time. Spirit precedes matter and informs all its manifestations (see, for example, 'The Ensouled Rock' below). Over the past century and a half we have reached a turning-point in our long evolution, at which this long immersion of the mind in its physical matrix has cut off our view of the spiritual dimensions out of which we have condensed.

This juncture is critical and its possible outcomes by no means certain. The assumed materialism of most modern thinking is both a stage in our legitimate evolution and a pathological vector that besets it. If not redressed by a reawakened consciousness of our spiritual genealogy, it will descend further into a quasi-autistic fugue of self immured in its own well of self-consciousness, unable to apprehend or relate to a cosmos it perceives as wholly foreign. The many ramifications of Steiner's thought, which have by turns eluded, infuriated, and intrigued me for decades since I first encountered them in the late 1980s, cannot be reduced to tidy prose summary, so I won't try. What little I've said here should serve to illuminate those aspects of these poems that draw on anthroposophical inspirations.

For a collection that stands under the title *The Gnostic Hotel*, a brief word about Gnosticism is in order as well. The term names a turn of thought that rose like a pervasive scent in the centuries immediately on either side of Christ's advent. Its teachings are diffuse and varied, inflecting the thought of Judaism, Christianity and, later, Islam, as well as the Neoplatonic philosophy that was a more or less default posture for anyone engaging with big questions about life, the universe and everything in the Mediterranean world around the time of Christ. Gnosticism remained a fringe phenomenon, declared a heresy by Christianity's doctrinal authorities and formally rejected by the heirs of Platonic tradition, among them the most famous of late-classical philosophers, Plotinus.

It's not hard to see why. Gnosticism was naturally contrarian, declaring, in effect (and well in advance of Groucho Marx), 'Whatever it is, I'm against it'. It turns traditional texts and doctrines on their heads. The gnostic perspective reads the God of Genesis as a cosmic gaoler, casting spirits into limiting bodies of clay, and reveres that story's serpent as a bringer of saving wisdom. It sees life on earth as a botch, a catastrophic detour onto which human souls were lured from their original station in spiritual realms, down into the lower material reaches of creation by an agency it names in Greek as the *demiourgos*, the 'demiurge'. The word commonly means 'maker' or 'craftsman' but was transvalued by Gnosticism to suggest something more like 'counterfeiter', 'trickster', or 'con-man'. An intelligence 'on the make', as it were. In Gnostic-Christian terms, the demiurge is a fallen angel in whom pride has fostered the delusion that he in fact *is* the creator, like someone today declaring himself Napoleon or Jesus. To prove it he creates a world (*our* world, thank you very much) but gets it hopelessly wrong, like a five-year-old's rough sketch of the Taj Mahal. Evil, disease, death and predation, along with everything else that makes characters like Job, Ecclesiastes or Melville's Captain Ahab denounce their worlds as monstrous affronts to both reason and virtue, are all attributed to the demiurge's malice or simple incompetence. Ever after he remains preoccupied with keeping the rest of us from noticing his fraud, like the Wizard of Oz bellowing that we 'pay no attention to the man behind the curtain!' The valiant Gnostic is a freedom fighter, seeking to bat away the veils of illusion cast by the demiurge. Fans of *The Matrix* will immediately recognise its gnostic inspiration. Steiner himself was sympathetic to the insights of Gnosticism, though he did not subscribe to them in their entirety, and Anthroposophy has often been mistakenly dismissed as a revival of the old gnostic heresy.

Anyone who's experienced the kind of disillusion or devastation that stings us to exclaim, 'Stop the world, I want to get off', has reached the gnostic brink. Most of us will have a good cry and then just get on with things. In our default modernity, walled off from the spiritual realities that might afford alternative perspectives, what else can we do? Everything that makes us recoil from, say, a terminal disease as an existential error, as something wrong with the world rather than mere biology or physiology, is an echo of the Gnostic's resistance to the givens of this world. *I'm not having it.* Gnostics believe they have seen through the world's shoddy pretences. They 'know' the score, hence the name given their tendency, *gnosis*, a Greek word that means 'knowledge'.

The etymological roots of 'hotel' give us other words as well: 'hostel', 'host' (both master of ceremonies and armed force), 'hospice', 'hospital', 'hospitality', and 'hostile'. The guest can be a ghost that leaves you aghast. A visitant, not from around these parts. No one belongs in a hotel: workers and guests alike lead their real lives elsewhere. Their paths cross fortuitously in a space built only for passage *through*. Home lies somewhere beyond the visible horizon. The disgruntled child may take refuge in a fantasy that he or she was adopted and is, unbeknownst to all, genuine royalty fallen on fairy-tale hard times. Sufficiently provoked, we're all closet Gnostics.

        We hope you enjoy your stay . . .

Geworfenheit: The Gnostic Hotel

The German word means 'thrown-ness' or 'the state of being thrown', used by the twentieth-century philosopher Martin Heidegger to denote the condition of human consciousness amidst the cognitive and epistemological swirls of incarnate existence. Picture a punch-drunk cartoon boxer, with tweeting birds and stars circling his lolling head. Or, if you like, Milton's Satan in Book 1 of Paradise Lost, *coming to as he bobs on the lake of fire in hell after his infinitely long fall from heaven. Kerplunk . . .*

Few now can read our alien ancestry,
our ineluctable otherness that tells
of elsewhere origins, primordial swerve
of fall, transgression, borders strayed across
that mark our exit, exile, exodus.
The castaway who makes his isle a home
may sink in comfort to forgetfulness
yet still be lost. We bear our checks and woes –
the hurricane that shreds our woven hut,
the rising seas that whelm our sandy dot,
the homesick melancholy sigh at dusk.
Each minds us of our lost identity.
And though its recollection score the heart
with desolation and ache of phantom limbs,
far better such remorse than ease that lulls
our swimming heads to deeper loll and nod.

The wake-up calls may startle and affront,
and we may curse the chirpy clerk downstairs,
but she, with ruthless kindness and aplomb,
is only meeting our last night's request,
that we left at the desk when we checked in
(*did* she say her name was Sophie then?),

guests of the obliging demiurge,
glad for a roof so far away from home,
but needing no velour and potted palms
to dress the facts of circumstance collapsed
upon our pinched-off selves: check-out time
indefinitely delayed till we recall
just where we left that missing set of keys.

Agency

Who writes these notes that turn up every day
in bottles screwed halfway into the sand?
He's got a pile of messages and glass,
the latter many-coloured, bearing names
from far-off lands and tongues. Each scrap they hold
he could have penned himself – by happy chance,
since dictionaries don't grow thick out here.
He reads them, yet, though every word speak true,
they semaphore some thought he can't unpack.
He shuffles scraps to sort and rearrange,
hoping they'll betray the far-off minds
who pitched them bottle-folded to the sea.
But why should bottles land here every day,
as though the waves played postman to his door?
Not one was ever signed, though if it were
he'd dare not look too near, for fear the name
he'd find there at the bottom were his own.

Psyops: y/n

This war knows neither dusty streets nor bombs.
The lanes we scout shade subtler enemies,
threading outlaw quarters of our minds
where improvised explosives detonate
in eerie silence – tear no flesh nor bone,
yet shred the will and lacerate the heart
that surgeon never stitched by theatre light.

In mental trenches, spirits hand-to-hand
wield daggers of despair and mutiny,
insurgents since before the lurch of time
sent seismic shudders down creation's spine.

Here we leapt in, like paratroopers dropped
behind the lines, not knowing what we'd find
nor what would find us, tasked but to repeat
our names stamped onto golden ID tags,
till they be so inscribed upon our souls
before the fate of all that moves descends
to swat us from the play of board and piece.

GAME OVER. DO YOU WANT TO PLAY AGAIN?
y/n

Nomenclature: A Gnostic Sleigh-Ride

SPIRIT breathes the freedom of the air
to SOUL's in-marrowed, barrowed, harrowed dance
beneath the caul of FLESH that beds its dare
to venture on a sleigh-ride circumstance
across a lifetime's stretch of broken swerves.
A bumpy ride dispels *Geworfenheit*
from swimming head and backside's singing nerves.
Harpoons sit on Leviathan upright,
like quills upon the fretful porpentine
whose taut lines slash the riders through each swell,
concussed by peak and trough grown dark as wine
as twilight swallows sky, a final well.
    The monster's spine still ploughs the waves ahead
    until it sounds to seek the sunken dead.

Nella Selva Oscura: **The Demiurge**

The busy world unscrolls along my screen
in YouTube thumbnails, feeds of every sort,
all pulsing with reality's bright sheen.
But all abstracted, thinned, displayed to sport
with eyes unmoored by minds unschooled to look
past hands that hold out sticks for us to fetch,
distracted from the contents of a book
to gape upon its cover, pixel-sketch
sufficient to approximate a scene
we enter, like lost children in a wood,
a candy cottage: gingerbread canteen
whose curtains' marzipan volutions hood
   the figure at the iron stove inside
   who stokes the fires lit for us to ride.

The Gnostic Labyrinth

   Souls body-slammed to unforgiving floors,
lashed by indifferent lines of time and space
in rooms with onyx ceilings and no doors,
   where consciousness must hunker down in place
to hide from hostile eyes and not be caught,
at once locked down yet cast adrift to pace
   the lengths of fractal corridors in thought,
whose winding coils enmesh incarnate mind,
a labyrinth no Daedalus has wrought,
   where errant reason leaves each passage mined
with elemental traps of cause adduced
and ineluctable effect divined.
   A self-wrought maze and slalom, down which, sluiced
like torrents through the turbines of a dam,
we serve our captors' ends, are never loosed
   while caught within the whirling cosmic glam,
the clockwork play of sphere round nested sphere
that reads our fortunes like some fairground scam.
   Star-flung foundlings, lost and prey to fear
of what this headlong rush through time may bring,
we dance to our doom, the circumstantial leer
   of all the stuffs and properties that ring
our narrow stalls hoots brazen mockeries,
a colosseum mob whose voices spring
   to cry the swift dispatch of casualties –
their living forms, made meat, weigh on the sand,
such entertainments wrung from agonies
   as we the players cannot understand,
but hail the demiurge's curtain call

with slurred *nos morituri*[1] wave of hand
   and so to business, backed against the wall,
to dodge the *retiarius*' tangled net
until we're trussed, sent rolling down the hall
   to bide what comes, what fortune will beget
upon our flailing flesh and wandering wit:
then bed, as dreams will come and suns will set.

---

[1] From the gladiators' salute to the emperor before their combats: *nos morituri te salutamus* ('We who are about to die salute you').

BY THE WATERS OF BABYLON

i. The Babylonian Exile

A Verrazzano-Narrows Meditation

'Paumanok' *is a native name for Long Island, the fish-shaped island that carries the New York City boroughs of Brooklyn and Queens in its head and, halfway along its belly, the township of Babylon where I was born in 1957 and where Walt Whitman taught at a local high school in 1835-36. Whitman makes frequent use of* 'Paumanok' *to name Long Island in his* Leaves of Grass. *The Verrazzano-Narrows Bridge was the world's longest suspension bridge when it was completed in 1964. It joins Brooklyn to the separate island borough of Staten Island and is the route off Long Island for travellers to the mid-Atlantic east coast of the United States. In 1978 I crossed it on my way to begin the rest of my life off the island where I first hit the ground.*

I fell to earth in Babylon – Long Island,
not the ancient Mesopotamian state.
Just a major commuter terminus
along the south shore of fish-shaped Paumanok
out of Penn Station, changing at Jamaica
as often as not. I grew up there and left
for parts unknown (to me and mine at least)
for reasons sound but later open to doubts:
study and love primarily, none of which
fell out quite as I'd planned, but that's okay –
where else should I be but where I am?
But now I've made a half-turn round the world,
its bulk looms large between my then and now
and some days I reflect on all I've left
so far away, family and friends, of course,
but other things as well: identities

I bore for certain spells and put aside,
personae strung upon a golden thread
stretched like the Verrazzano-Narrows Bridge:
its hither pier sunk in my infant squalls,
its span arched over clutching fingers of cloud,
thrumming, tensed against its farther end,
as winds from off the ocean's boundless reach
bow melodies upon its length that sing
of the home my fall left dwindling between my heels.

ii. Early Morning Departure Lounge

These are the hours of darkness, these the times
dispatching us with swift efficiency
toward some end we can't anticipate,
the eastern glow a dawn or furnace-mouth.
We hear the rumble of machinery
beneath our feet, the travelator's hum
as rollers pass below the walkway's flat.
From terminal to terminal we glide,
in transit over lands debatable,
where neither monsters nor enchanters be,
where voices, after Babel, polyglot,
inform us quietly of gates and states,
the weathers of this space that owns no sky
but feeds us one by one to its domain.

iii. Emigré

In this strange city, he takes his usual seat
at his usual table, while men and women pass,
their every glance and footstep purposeful.
He nurses cooling coffee, jots some lines
in a notebook perched upon one knee that's crooked
across the other. His hat-brim shades the page.
He has no business being here at all;
his home lies far away, beneath the thump
of mobs patrolling ways that he once walked,
in freedom that demanded only air
and light that strewed fair scenes about his feet.

iv. Building Babylon

Why poetry? For, as you probably know,
that medium has rarely earned its crust
since markets and transactions rose to claim
the final word on all we hold of worth.
Oh, museums stash scattered gems. Libraries too.
But step back, hold your hands out, make a frame
around the CBD of any city.
What do you see? Chaldean towers and spires,
Babylonian ziggurats stacked high,
once trained upon the skies, transvalued now
to corporate entelechies – what *corpora*
do they incorporate? What need to say?
Bankers' butts, executives devote
to management of abstract assets bled

from toil of muscle, mind, imagination
refracted through the ratios of machines
to radiant spread-sheet splendour, pure and sure,
calculated to a nicety.

How does that consort with meaning's play,
that dances like some Tinkerbell to lure
you further into dim uncertainties?
'What's *that*?' 'Dunno. It could be anything'.
That's no way to build a topless tower.
No fixed address, just wandering by the way –
but that's where Meaning lives, her cousins Truth
and Wisdom too. You've got to *follow* them.
They won't be hailed and hauled or made to march,
though they might set *you* skipping double time.
What architect, on fire for ziggurats,
could tolerate such wayward *jeux d'esprit*?
Stones can't dance if you want to pile 'em high,
but some say Merlin wove a haunted song
to waltz the liths of Stonehenge to their round.

v. The *Makaris*
a reply to 'Building Babylon'

Why poetry? I ask again, because
the temper of our age bewilders thought
that grapples at close quarters with such stuff,
fiercer of reply than Jacob's angel.
'Who', I might as well have asked, 'are *you*?'
Poetry knows, but, mostly out of kindness,
will not tell. We need her desperately.

Case in point: an advertisement screened
across the many windows of our trams.
An outsized *ingenue* with orange hair
beneath a rakish hat, before a mic,
posing soulfully, guitar in hand
(old Fender Coronado, should you care)
in public transport, midmost flight of song.
The slogan, *we're for the makers*, blazed for us
by a bank, ostensibly keen to lend a hand
to builders, businesses and keening waifs.
The makers! Words to conjure up the soul
of William Dunbar, who catalogued the deaths
of his kind, the *makaris* who wove with words,
though none can say if Dunbar made his plaint
for poets, poetry, or for himself –
wee, timorous mousie under the beady eye
of death who has no ear for well-turned feet,
squeaking *timor mortis conturbat me*.

But that was long ago. My point today
is *for the makers*, solemnly intoned
by a *bank*, for crying out loud. Makers of *what*?
Of readies for their coffers, obviously:
the slogan-slingers no more discriminate
fine melody than ass-eared Midas. Soul,
as figured in that singer's stagey pose,
serves here as velcro for the eye, a hook
or barbed harpoon that sticks 'The Bank of Melbourne'
into mental blubber like Queequeg's shaft.

Again, why poetry? Just look around.
Death, whose taste for poet gave Dunbar the willies,

has not relented in his ministry
and plies his trade amongst all living forms
with his wonted gusto. Take language: long ago,
in Athens, fast and loose, the rhetors played
their word-games, horribly familiar now:
language wielded tool-wise for results
with scant regard for inconvenient truths.
Tongue-twisting parliamentary *savoir-faire*,
the limbo-dance of lawyer's wiggle-speak,
the ad-man's pitch, the Ministry of Truth,
alternative facts, words angled and deployed
to jimmy the locks securing reasoned thought.

In the beginning Word, but in this latter dark,
a carnival of hucksters' lurid booths:
imposture, imprecision, tactical scorn
for anyone sufficiently worked up
to have a go at baring all the lies,
which lie in plainest, fullest light of day,
unfussed and unembarrassed, drawling 'Whaat?'
with smirk and shrug, dismissive swipe of hand,
'I got a million! Don't be such a loser'.
Sloganeering set to auto-repeat.
No thought required – just add air and heat.

While in the other corner we behold
the challengers, already black and blue
with pummelling and, to tell the honest truth,
looking just a little worse for wear:
the journalists and intellectuals,
of olden days the arbiters of fact,
not without their own chicaneries
pursued from time to time to circulate

more copy, snaffle tenure or the clicks
in website weirs where everybody goes
to find their fortune now. But worse the fate
of windborne speech itself, that beats its wings
like dove in bell-jar vacuum. The air that bears
all thought from mind to mind ebbs from the sky.
Might as well go home and wait for night.
What angel can announce, what tongue can bless,
find purchase in its oral cavity
to shake the solemn blissful sheets of speech
like wonder-wings of cloud upon the winds,
that veil and bare the peaks of unscaled thought,
the open hand of language raised to say,
'I hear you, Sister. Brother, I can see
the flicker of that fire behind your eyes'.
Thus the poets sang, the *makaris*
of every tongue once lit beneath the moon.
But now their craft retreats to far-off heights,
in learned halls, arts council-grant *débats*,
and bookshop wine-and-nibbles gatherings
of *cognoscenti* few and far between.
While the world below swims thick with morbid prose,
online chatter scarcely worth our while
to flag as belly-up linguistic act,
from every quarter sown like pestilence,
spewed from digital servers, made to play
as instruments for those who seek to draw
the leverage of mere spectacle and click.
They shuffle stones upon the plain in heaps,
ascend no heights nor plumb resounding depths,
beneath a sky that weathers do not touch,
its grey a cloudless nullity that shows
no sun by day, no starry vault by night,

where mind, untouched by meaningful event,
can only circle its own echoes, self
enclosed upon its own foreshortened shore,
to heap the sand into no battlements.
What word can resonate across such waste?
Tongueless vacuum, impotent silence reign –
none to stir, no air to carry calls,
sans voice, *sans* song, *sans* light, *sans* everything.

vi. New Year's Day: Wisdom in Exile

Her light falls dim, and eyes and blossoms close
in night that answers to no swelling day.
Her name is torn. In rags she turns the mills
of calculation, forced to tot up stones,
enumerating ratios of truth,
while men with heads and loins and tongues of bulls
engorge and riot in her hall. Their reeks
obscure the tessellated floor and smudge
the luminous geometry of her dance.

Its turns still fascinate the labyrinth
of our dreams. There yet we catch a glimpse of her
beneath a vacant sky: her robe pulled close,
her face invisible but for her eyes
whose beams now find no soul on whom to light,
in whom her voice may sound its wonted laugh,
with whom her feet might once more step in time.

Far off the palace revelries still bray.
She pauses; does not turn to see her home

left desolate, subject to loud affront.
She summons down no curse but takes her way,
her absence sure to conjure greater woe
than any malediction could pronounce.

No search through street or field or wilderness
will turn up any trace of her. Her steps
conduct to circles beyond the planets' weave,
while we can only watch the house she built
begin its final ruinous collapse,
whence none survive, perhaps, to bear the tale.

GNOSTIC LIFE IN WARTIME

i. *Realitätsprinzip*

Triumph's shards in squalid shambles struck:
abattoirs of bodies crushed and torn,
bones disclosed beneath the sun to warn
the waking soul of matter's fearsome ruck.
The pageantry we took for glory's fame,
crowns' carats, ounces troy and fairy floss
a thorny wreath on bloodied head, soul's loss,
a sordid jakes of defeated shame.
What once we hailed as victory plants boots
in swamp and desert folly lost to shame,
stale foetor of such excremental fame,
hero's honour noised as monkey-hoots.
   We see now only what the lens reveals:
   surface compost ground by clockwork wheels.

ii. The Scholar Sentinel

He stands his watch both sides of winter night:
farewells the sun's last fading-ember gleam
and waits to hail its first blush on the seam
where sky and earth unfold horizon's bight
and light steals round the corner like a thief,
its aura whispering of soon-blown day
not yet unfurled, but surely on its way,
stand-down notice, hinted-at relief.

Between, the labour: study, scribal crawl
by eye and quill across the parchment's weft,
the spoor of ink both taken up and left
as he beats the bounds along creation's wall,
   ramparts flung to weather chaos' wrath
   that its domain should shoulder watchman's path.

iii. Trench Warfare

Who then will keep the shadow-hordes at bay?
No fence, no wall, no barrier can stay
that unrelenting press upon our thought,
whose culverts have admitted them unfought,
unseen and unsuspected, barrow-moles
who undermine foundations, towers, souls:
the death-watch beetles in the panelling,
their mandibles' relentless channelling
of entropy that saps our hearts' resolve
to pump the currents of our thoughts' evolve.

But who then can descend that inner stair?
Behind the door most pass by unaware
or with a shiver they dismiss as nerves,
with eyes averted as awareness swerves
away from thresholds bidding it below
to hear the night-cock rear its head to crow
from its inverted perch on basement beam.
What harrowing could here break heaven's gleam
to turn those pioneers along their sap,
transpose their laid petards from hell to hap?

Such servants must dig deep: no loud parade
in public square sun-blazed, but in the shade
of hidden trial, obscure perplexity,
to beat the bounds of hell's concavity.
No influence, no Facebook posts, no tweets,
no recognition on the vacant streets
of under-towns where only ghosts process
through nightmare cellars of each home's address,
that topside shows a cottage neat and trim,
all unaware what serpents writhe within.

iv. *Das Boot*

The love that is/is not delves farthest down
when, like a depth-charge, left to ply its power
invisibly in ocean's unlit bower,
it sinks to blossom fatally, a crown
of shock-wave passions blanching swells' blue cheeks.
Quiet follows. Oil slick. Flotsam's toss
that tell of hope's implode below, of loss
of structural integrity, great leaks
through every plate and pipe of mind's defence,
black water's rise through gangway's shrill alerts
and strobing lights, though none can mend the hurts
and silent cold unstrings the living's tents,
    now struck that they may wander different ways
    beneath nor sky nor sea, unthread the maze.

v. No Man's Land

Space is matter's backwash, rucked and turned

by its insistence on itself, as time
whips winds whose waves have carved its brow and burned
through veins of ore, in fists of coal and lime.
Thus stars consume themselves, and thus we curl,
like papers, incandescent in the blaze
we feed like frantic diplomats who hurl
incriminating minutes of our days
into the furnace, toss their awkward scrawl
that tells of dereliction, false desires,
of how our progress stuttered to a crawl
and left our bones in khakis strung on wires
   that space and time draped over no-man's land,
   where hopes turn stone and stones dissolve to sand.

vi. Earnest of Game

Where is the governour of this gyng?[1]
   Sir Gawain and the Green Knight. I.224-225

Talk not to me of blasphemy, man; I'd strike the sun if it insulted me.
   Ahab to Starbuck in *Moby Dick*, 'The Quarter-Deck'

To stay the governor who's come unstuck,
mad skipper at the helm who spins the wheel:
a gambler set on calling chance to heel,
fixation by some mental lightning struck.

To rescue souls from rabbit holes: but how?

---

[1] The Green Knight, having just crashed Arthur's court, interrupts the Christmas party in progress and crudely demands, 'Where is the governor of this gang?' i.e. 'Who's in charge of this rabble?'

That quarterdeck stands deep in thought's recess,
festooned with severed rigging and the mess
of sodden canvas thrown from stern to prow.

Yet what authority have we to wield,
we punch-drunk sailors flung across the boards?
The planks whipped from beneath our feet, the cords
of lanyards snapped and all our stays unreeled.

Our anchor claws the seabed rock in vain,
our purchase lost, our keel an unstrung kite.
Sauve qui peut? An elemental flight
through sky upended, which-way slashing rain.

And still our crazed commander at the con
defies the tempest, bawls his hoarse inane
to lash the spirits of this hurricane
and laughs to see the waterspouts' pavane.

Gnostic Interrogatives

Why now? Why here? Why not then and there?
Why any time and place below the sun?
Who banished me beneath this flesh I bear?
Who multiplied my thoughts but left me one?
What finds me at Cartesian triple 0?
What answers to my name in sleeper's roll?
What lies on either side, above, below
this dizzy summit thrust up from the hole
of pure non-entity? And where was I
before I came upon myself up here?
A meeting fraught as any check-point cry
of 'Halt!' and 'Papers, please!' Whose stealth? Whose fear?
   Existence throws whole worlds around your head
   and bids you skip just this side of the dead.

Debutante

Her name's Sophia? I have known her just
the length of these poor lines I've spun to snare
some spicules of her iridescent dust
like sun and dew on spider's spiral flare.
Yet she has waved her pennons overhead
since I began to raise my infant view
to contemplate celestial glories spread
in constellations I could not construe.
And yet I felt my depths begin to rise
with intimations I could scarcely squeak:
burgeoning in light slung from the flies
as I took my first steps, began to speak
   such lines as I had studied long before
     in the tiring house beyond the farthest shore.

Learning Curve

We haven't yet discerned this simple fact:
the great majority of our machines,
from flint to fire to wheel to newest chip,
enlarge the boundaries of death's domain
still further, stealing into living lands,
reclaiming for the inarticulate sea
those acres once worked over by the plough
to bear abundant fruit beneath the sun.
Now furrows puzzle lobsters in the dark
as porpoises and stingray float where crows
once flocked to hear the ploughman's clear refrain.

His plough was a machine, of course, that bound
the work of lever and point to oxen's heft –
more acreage churned, more deeply, evenly,
that tilth might thrive and yields swell bin and barn.
Yet tell me when the good of bumper crops
became a god unto itself, devote
to abstract profit turned with Midas' touch:
gold apples, grains and daughters stashed in banks.

The wheel can swallow distance, mill your flour,
helm a ship or entertain a child.
But tell me how to sift from that the crash
of Rameses', Homer's or Boudicca's chariots,
or the yearly highway mess we just accept
as necessary carnage, collateral
against the loan of speed from here to there,
which we equate with progress.
                              Surely fire,
kept firmly under lock and key in hearth

and factory furnace, serves its masters well?
Until it doesn't, as we have only just
begun to fathom fully as the coal
and oil we suck from underneath the soil
now charge the earth with their Cretaceous heat,
as if the centuries of bursting bombs,
the torches of inquisitors and mobs
and Neronic arson had sounded no alarms.

The children got by the Wrights upon the sky
now hurtle death from padded-seat command:
the Reapers' wheels and fire lashed and loosed
on heads pricked down by algorithmic lot –
the word itself a bitter irony,
sprung from the tongue whose speakers nursed the arts
of mathematics when our ancestors
still calculated in Roman numerals.

To be completely frank, it's no good look.
I could go on: what bitter alchemy
taught Cain a better use for field-stone waste,
to end fraternal quarrels with a bang?
Imagination deals both life and death,
but we don't know which way to point the thing
or what live round might snug inside the chamber.
It's always fun till somebody gets hurt,
and we wield scant discretion in this game,
compulsive Russian roulette in reverse:
for every gain, five losses. Every light
casts shadows we can't even start to count.
Each footfall echoes down dark corridors,
encrypted passageways we can't resist,
that wind us deeper in creation's bowels.

Signs of the Times

Lasciate ogni speranza, voi ch'entrate.
     Dante, *Inferno* III.9

Mobs and markets, brigands, mountebanks –
raggedy figures flit the city squares
like fugitives whose uprising has failed:
one glimmering of hope, then only choice
of flight or brave despair: 'I'm Spartacus!'
The crosses line the *Via Appia*
and all roads string the charnel daisy-chains
from here to Rome, where empire squats in purple,
rank and ravenous and keen for sport.

Elsewhere, night beneath a troubled sky.
The sun recedes and shadows drape the land
like shrouded furniture that crowds the floor
beneath the trussed-up ballroom chandeliers
in a house closed down for winter. Memory
of love alone can insulate the heart
against the frost that gropes to numb and still.
It sidles forward, into its misgivings,
keen to get the wretched business over,
to face the worst, to bluff and blunder past
what horrors hang in future time's deep stores.

The jeers and hoots let fly from souls convinced
of one idea that's digitally dinned
from every quarter till no other sounds.
The sneers at all that speaks for charity,
paraded to the rail to walk the plank
by pirate crews who trample governance

in tailored suits bespoke from spread-sheet cloth
by cutlasses of ideology.
Walpurgisnacht Shabbat we've seen before,
on far too many similarly botched
occasions when some lie put on a mask
and thronged the streets with raucous carnival
whose pageants traced the circle-walk of hell.
Not noticing the drop, blind to the walls
whose steep, sheer sides rise every way to bar
the ways that might lead back to light and air.

How can simple words unlace this spell,
when they themselves are trussed and pitched
like cannonballs to shatter battlements?
What gardener sow goodly, patient seed
that might take hold as meaning, bear rich fruit
beneath the present's scything entropy?
Mere argument prolongs the agony:
forensics foster mechanoid exchange,
clay pigeons pulled and shattered in mid-flight.
Nothing to see here . . . please move along.

Motley, choice absurdity alone
has any chance of telling any truth
but telling it slant, like Shakespeare's fools and clowns,
to dodge the serried ranks of ministers,
of pundits, politicians and panjandrums,
committees, councils, deliberative plods,
to open eyes to the emperor's stark lack,
sartorial-deficient, unrelieved
by Adam and Eve's redeeming modesty.
They at least displayed shame's decency,
quaint nicety beyond these braggart crews

who let hang out what most should prompt their shame.

Can any say for sure where all this tends?
We hardly need Elijah's frown to see
the skies ahead all wearing ugly looks.
So let it rip . . . these thugs and sots demand
some sharp comeuppance. How, and when, if ever?
There's only hope of doors thrown open wide,
to let sun flush the deepest nooks and holes
as all stand inside-out upon that day,
full selves revealed in pocket-lint, stray coin.

End-Times Etiquette

Then yff man shall saye unto you: lo, here is Christ, or there is Christ: believe it not: for there shall arise falce christes, and falce prophetes and shall geve greate signes and wonders. So greatly that yff it were possible, even the chosen shulde be brought into erroure.

        Matthew 24:23-24 (Tyndale's translation)

The trick is NOT to found some doomsday cult,
but walk beneath this dimming sun and give
what good you can to those whose paths cross yours.
Avoid the hoo-hah; keep your own voice calm.
So many different generations brayed
the End of Days had caught them by the scruff,
but, to be honest, today has copped the look,
as believers throw themselves beneath the wheels
of the latest demagogue's bus. Or Gog-Magog's.

A death-wish rattles in our culture's throat,
the hubbub fanned and spread by Facebook meme.
Chicken Little, eyes glued to the sky,
bolts straight toward the fox's gaping maw.
That's not to say no fractures chip the blue,
or Reynard past the wire is just fake news.
Something's up, but no one's got a clue
how rough a beast is slouching, even now,
toward its date with brick-wall destiny.

To call it self-fulfilling prophecy
is true, but no one's listening, those least
who egg it on by fervour or design,
too busy machinating or praise-Godding

to see their car has veered the wrong way round,
accelerating down toward that brink.
The profiteers peel off with pockets lined,
while true believers steel for rapturous flight,
beyond the reach of gravity or fact,
superbly unaware how eerily
that boof-head clown to whom they've lent the wheel
has mastered the arts of an apprentice beast.

Taurus Minor in *Ellorhwær*

In Otherwhere, beside the House of Play,
the empty whizzers slow, and vacant swings
still sway as if abandoned in mid-flight. The dust,
kicked up by feet that just now hit the ground,
still drifts on air that rings with fading cries
of children lost to sight. The sunlight bars
the track of their retreat with gilded beams.
Let echoes die. Attendance not required.

The trailing hems of garments everywhere –
loose threads like Ariadne's, to be tugged
along unravelled lengths that twist and turn,
the maze that swallowed you so long ago,
and after rolled in balls that circle suns
whose fire warms other grounds, whose cursive paths
spell riddles other than that chestnut posed
by the Sphinx's tired stand-up badinage.

Demobbed to a petting zoo, she tolerates
the hands and coos of children not yet bound
to sally forth upon the ways and find
new playgrounds whose equipment stands in need
of careful maintenance. There's time enough
to carry will between the hedgerows, where
the murmuration's starlings roost well hid
until the sky shakes out their billowed folds.

Kenosis: The Dirigible of Hermes Psychopompos

Kenosis *is a Greek word that means 'emptying'. In theological and philosophical discourses it can refer to God's divesting himself of his divine attributes to take on Christ's human nature or, more broadly, the divine turning out a pocket of its omnipresence to make room for the cosmos it wishes to create. At the end of Chaucer's* Troilus and Criseyde, *Troilus' soul is led to the outermost of the celestial spheres nested around the world, whence he looks down on the scene of all his excruciations, reduced by distance to a moist green dot, and laughs.*

A loss portaged too far across dry land:
a young love lightning-flashed to splash its light
across the architecture of the heart,
its arches, geodesics, vaults and domes;
its colonnades and porticoes arrayed;
its groins that quarter heaven's own expanse.
All thrown in high relief by one brief flare
no sooner glimpsed than gone, lost cries alone
left echoing across the vacancy
to gauge how far the freezing void had spread
on every hand toward infinity.

Scooped and hollowed out, the vasty deep
balloons the more the more souls thrash about,
circumferences displacing every centre:
mere vacancy that yawns, a strip-mined gulf,
upon whose lip each sits and mourns long years,
until some spin of cosmos, heart or thought
upends the scene: all that concavity
turned cavern, arched impossible above.

Light spills from overhead, across the floor
of one enormous hangar, barn-wide doors

uncoupling outward to admit the day
from which a quicksilver dirigible sinks down.
Cetacean of the sky, it noses in
and fills completely all that hollowness,
buoyed up by all the air that it's displaced.

The gondola hatch swings free. The pilot waves,
an enigmatic smile across his face.
The other hops aboard. They back and rise.
He watches the world receding far beneath,
each planetary sphere concentrically
sent down behind like escalator floors,
transecting the departments, cosmic goods
of every kind placed temptingly on show.
He throws out all he'd bought on his way down,
his memory of that trip just then restored,
as they shed yet more weight at every stage.
They cross the ecliptic, dodge the ram and bull,
careful to look both ways, up and down:
beneath, the planets' nested gyroscopes,
above, the moveless stars immutable,
and there the oblate spheroid finds its place,
along the phosphorescent Milky Way.
He turns his gaze below and laughs and laughs.

The Divorce of Mind and Matter

When at last Descartes sheared mind from dirt,
he'd no idea how matter would crowd mind
and its associates – spirit, soul and god –
into a disused corner of our thought,
there to gather dust like outgrown toys.

Meanwhile, matter, which never had before
known such a sense of its own push and heft,
began to throw its weight around down here,
until poor mind got everything back-to-front
and had forgotten its old sovereignty.

They'd worked together for uncounted years,
mind the lantern, teacher, crossing-guard,
but matter yielded only to more force,
to bodies shoving bodies from their path,
so it of course assumed all else did too.

Thus mind became a ghost, an airy nought,
all its illuminations just a play
of light and shadow, nothing you could touch,
and no substantial player in the world,
whose stuff now clings like mud to haul us down.

The Errant Knight

It's in the name: all wanderers will stray,
the errant knight commits his share of bads –
it's not all pricking horseback o'er the plain.
Shit happens, things go wrong, so much awry.
Illusions dupe the eye, enchantments throw
cream pies as well as glams across the room,
barbs and bouquets, thumps and wind's caress.
From time to time his path admits a grace,
entirely unasked-for, fair and free,
until the chained events throw him again.

The proper hero learns the shrugging off
of life's humiliations. These can teach
if looked at squarely – never mind your blush
of pure chagrin for that quixotic splat.
The trick of it is learning to avoid
the same old, same old pratfalls, jars and jeers.
Repeated jokes grow lame, and, from the wings,
the orchestrators of your vaudeville act
seem never at a loss for jolly japes
to keep the whole show flying when you flag.

So carry on, keep smiling, never mind
how often you get stretched upon your back,
while dust drifts slow across your sprawling limbs
and from the pit the brassy trumpeters
wave hats in front of wawing descant laughs.
One day perhaps they'll get your fanfare right,
tarantara-ing you through heaven's gates.

Garden Lore

Roll that stone once more across the tomb.
Show's over here; there's nothing more to see.
Go back to life as lived and death as died
and try to keep them separate in your dreams.
You may not find it simple anymore.
Outliers of each now scout the other's patch,
their yin-yang growing fractal and unsure,
like milk stirred into coffee, like those souls
who wake so slowly, dozy, still enwrapped
in whatever scenes that bustling biddy sun
has goosed them from while they lay late abed.
The shadows deepen here above your heads,
while in the grave, unseen, a new light swells.

How do *I* know? You'll work it out, I guess.
Me? I'm just the gardener. Hired help.
No one special. Be careful of that rose!

Your Study in the Bardo

Death is not death: it's merely settling in
for a long winter's read of the book you wrote out *there*,
along the ways and weathers of the world,
before you crossed that threshold to sit *here*,
the armchair high-backed, buttoned, plush: the fire
a memory of toss and turn once borne,
now hearth-contained and warming face and toes.

The book is heavy, leather-bound like clothes
that God once fashioned for Adam and Eve's disgrace,
embossed with gilded letters that construe
a name both unfamiliar and your own.
The bread and wine laid out beside you clasp
the fires of old suns within their glow.
You understand them now, as, while you read,
the shapes whose contours you once lived appear
reversed and inside-out: the fathomless vale
that swallowed all your tears a mountain peak
that lifts your tireless steps toward the stars.

ORPHEUS AND EURYDICE
or, Hell's Harrowing Reconsidered

i. Farewell

The purple tartan shawl that wreathed her face,
the signs for 7th and W 14th obscured
by swirling snows above that last embrace
they leaned politely into, then adjured
each other to take care and fare you well.
They turned upon the ways they've followed since,
presence patched from word and thought, the bell
of dream rung once or twice, all sober hints
that distance holds desire against her will.
The years teach patience, a chastening of the soul
whose fidgets reason gentles to lie still
and play its part against the looming whole,
   whose measure neither she nor he can take,
   except as favour, for each other's sake.

ii. Not at Home

She's almost never there, but I don't mind:
I long ago grew used to her remove.
The distances of years and miles unwind
that skein of presence others think must prove
some fact of beauty, love's all-needful bound.
But fact and need are outliers at best,
the shabby suburbs of the lighted town
where all roads bend whose travellers invest
their uttermost breath to catch a fleeting scent,

part memory, part garden sprung from dream
that's never answered sun's diurnal bent
but wavers in the starlight's spectral gleam.
   She steps among those midnight blossoms' bells
   whose petals fan the lips of deeper wells.

iii. Scatterings

For pebbles flung against your upstairs sash,
I ask no pardon, only your ear turned
towards my beacon, lit with words whose ash
collects beneath these bonfires, which have burned
long times upon this moor, whose farthest blink,
expanding like the shattered fronts of stars,
speaks still, although their fires fell extinct
in ages past, beyond the harbour-bars.
Voice flung upon the wind like broadcast seed,
invisible assays of full-wrung thought,
pitched in bottles draped with trailing weed,
that seek your strand for you to find unsought.
   Like crystal pupae, amber, blue and green,
   they capsule morning for your waking scene.

iv. Absence Resolves

Madonna mia, I lack the means to say
how we might meet upon some other plane,
this twilight stirred and parted by new day
whose fire pours colours through each drop of rain,
transfigured tears, archival agonies
made yielding as the earth forgives the plough,

responds with grass that waves on every breeze.
The politesse of heaven can allow
forsaken seeds to send, from Hades' lee,
new shoots into the sun that none had guessed
could call their nodding heads above to see
day's pennons blazing on the morning's crest.
   No loss too sharp, no fall past remedy,
   no wound unstanched by secret ministry.

v. The Retired Mountaineer

Mere sentiment, long since reduced to ash,
can stake no values on external scenes:
a distant line of peaks whose weathers clash
in ghostly flickers, soundless sidelong sheens.
Their shadows do not fall this far across
the sun's sojourn along the sky's defiles.
Did I once wander there, concussed by loss
and tripping over tussocks, barred by stiles?
Horizons sag with memories whose weight
still leans upon the scales of my long thought.
Impressions stamped by sudden rock-fall fate
will stir the phantom limb to sing untaught.
   However indistinct, I can't unseat
   how earth showed from those summits at my feet.

vi. The Chymical Assay

You'd think I would have had enough by now –
in snippets edited by stingy clocks –

but inward acres answer to the plough
of retrospection hauled by memory's ox,
sidereal tilth that bears, by kindly sense,
mercurial quicksilver, iron from Mars,
venerean copper, lunar accidence
of silver hid with solar gold in bars,
Jovian tin and Saturn's pensive lead,
each feels its planet's fructifying touch,
a nuptial embrace upon earth's bed,
eluding miner's pick or miser's clutch.
   Thus your own *influenza*, from afar,
   rays down on me from your uncharted star.

The Fishers of Fissures

A silver line, dropped from some moonlit raft,
shines through the dark, held taut by leaden plumb
that weights one end to dangle down this shaft
and seek our lower sphere on heaven's thrum.
It plucks a melody our inner ear
discerns in depths of sleep or reverie.
The walls rise overhead, forbidding, sheer,
yet somewhere in that sky, love's deputies
patrol earth's shrunken face, a shrivelled ball,
its surface cracked where ocean boiled away,
and fissures gaped to swallow our each fall,
in pits where we've since lain past reach of day.
   Until we find ourselves reeled upwards, soft,
   by angel-anglers coaxing us aloft.

The Magi's Visitation

Dispatched to these far shores, beneath the trees,
we've watched the earth evolve, through stars entwined.
We've left the towers of Babylon behind,
for love alone set forth, crossed lands and seas.

Long years from where we started, we can see
how every clock concedes apocalypse:
all days are ripe, each measured moment snips
another sheer celestial biopsy,

cross-sectioned slices of our thought's traverse
of rise and fall along time's steep-pitched slopes
the second-hand a second hand that gropes
for purchase on the scree of Adam's curse.

In darker hues the body wears its scars,
a secret script of fortune's accident,
pegged down to stay the flesh as spirit's tent,
pink tabernacle, fox-hole in the wars,

the salient of psyche, self and soul,
whence they peer out across the rocky waste
where waves advance, retreat in sullen haste,
and spend their energy in futile roll.

A metamorphic alchemist's retort:
what shapes itself as first-day infant smile
shines upward from the feeding trough's defile.
Across this brink we peer and give report.

The Etheric Twist

Outward state unfolds from inward root,
but 'out' and 'in' cross at a single line,
a threshold where they twirl, exchanging masks,
the Moebius-self caught up in cosmic spray:
our inmost depths entangled with the stars.
As space, so time: the point-source of our births
in fact embedded in penumbral weave
of lives and destinies we cannot see
yet answer to in all desire and choice.

Psycho-mechanical meddling can't unpack
the densities of karma, fate and chance,
whatever airs and high degrees conferred
by college, university or school –
all addled by materialism's rip,
that bids to suck us, unawares, to sea,
to drown like Urizenic plates in baths
prepared by William, Catherine, and their sprites
to bid the rest of us swim between the flags.

On the Threshold

Expostulation
I can't remember when I fell to earth
and staggered under stone and gravity.
What angel sang the hour of my birth?
What king attended my nativity?
I've tuned an instrument that none will hear,
a stringed futility for carving air
in temporal excisions, sonic weir
across the stream of speech whose fish repair
to other haunts, evading my lame shifts
to tickle their insinuations home.
So what remains? I see only rifts
where they've escaped beneath the night's high dome.
   There I am due myself to make my way
   past moon's low pickets, sentinels of day.

Reply
Who knows how long ago he fell to earth,
to stagger under stone and gravity?
No angels sang the hour of his birth,
no kings attended his nativity.
He's lain down finally before a door
that's barred his every importunity,
crouched there, unravelled, enervate, and poor,
torn fingernails against its fixity.
What lies beyond? It's past his wit to say,
but he has dreamed: if he lean long enough,
he might hear hinges grind as they give way,
shrugged back like faded scales by serpent's slough,
a winding passage through the key-hole wards
that scrub him like a shuffled deck of cards.

Transcribal March

Ancient learning, very strangely worn:
its words borne on the writhing worm of tongue
in oral cavity, whence winds are sprung
to fall as letters, paper-bound and shorn

of voice and breath, transcribal mummery
of alphabet and codex, vellum, quill,
the armature of book and ink-pot spill,
where thought has ventured years in summary.

Yet now it strays between such lines to sound
what bustles in the hedgerows of the text,
turned boustrophedontic, ploughing meaning's next
emergence turned the other way around,

no mere galumph towards some finish line,
but spells that gather wayward powers held
by fine articulations, silken weld
of sound and sense in grammar's square and trine.

Speech performative sings past the scroll
of screen-wise mill-wheel rolling in the race
of reason's slow abrasions, grinding trace
of living kernels powdered for the dole

of sense in dull, discrete semantic bags.
Wisdom, on the hop, eludes such strain,
bows iridescent, nowhere in the rain,
refracting spectral pennons, ghostly flags.

Thus high upon the marches of the mind

the mental banners wave upon the airs.
Their speculative furlings rise like stairs,
in coruscations flung from soul's unbind.

The Smuggler

He steals across the borders, back and forth,
and bundles contraband beneath his tarps,
between polarities of south and north,
against the piercing twang of angels' harps.
But no one's fooled — his fondest subterfuge
lies bare-assed under heaven's golden eye.
Alarm-clock trumps will blast his sleep with huge
tarantara that summons him awry,
half-buttoned trousers flapping round his knees,
soul's *deshabillé*, scarce-decent show:
to stand before the ranks of watching trees
whose long attendance on the high and low
   served heaven better than his monkey-shines
   and stills, with silent dignity, his whines.

Blowback

With countless dragon's teeth the earth's been sown:
the dead, untimely or unjustly slain,
thrust unawares into the ether-zone,
bewildered by new night's appalling rain

that's sluiced the sun from heaven's capsized vault,
reversed the fabric of reality,
and left their senses dazed by an assault
that turns each convex to concavity.

Near and far trade places. Up and down
turn all upon its head. The sudden dead
of our empiric age lack means to sound
the contours they encounter: no sure lead

hangs taut to point out toes to swimming thought,
and your own words come spoken from afar
while others' well up from within unsought.
Time and space uncouple, doors ajar.

Baffled by this plunge from some to none,
they scrabble on the unfamiliar scree
and hunger for the rise and fall of sun,
with drowning swimmer's terror turn to flee.

They sense the living in a veiling mist,
but yearning only drives them farther off,
our own indifference tightens a cruel twist
of matter's blunt, indifferent shrug and scoff.

Our ignorance admits them to our minds:
like burglars forcing windows unsecured,
they blunder past our darkened, shuttered blinds,
impersonating thoughts we're self-assured

took shape within our heads. And thus they press
our moods and will into conformity
with their unfocused terrors, leaving us
a prey to bitter whim, gratuity

of unexamined will, not wholly ours,
ensures our best-laid plans *gang aft agley*.
And few anticipate what evil flowers
might sprout from seeds they sowed with best degree

of prudent forethought, whose outcomes will complete
the circle, pitching more across the brink,
whose wills press back on ours. There's no retreat:
we reap as we have sown. That simple link

we cannot apprehend and blunder on
through thickets dense with unmoored consequence,
the karmic blow-back, rumbling thunder on
our each horizon, warping our intents.

Signatures

    Soul wears soil as mask. As pure disguise?
As barrier to stay us from a drop?
As binding of its own descending sighs?
   All things our senses know serve as a strop
our reason's razor hones its edge against,
a trial surface, inside out, its top
    pulled through its bottom, held out taut and tense
that we might find sure footing in this world,
which otherwise would pass by in suspense
    like foggy tendrils, insubstantial, curled
back on themselves, recursions none would see,
unless they slap like heavy winds unfurled
    from Aeolus' cave, unrolling in their lee
the banners of a host's advance, unmarked –
the skylark's swerve, the breath that stirs the tree.
   The opened eye sees through the caul. The ark
once sheltered presence from the profane gaze,
as mind once veered through limitary dark,
    horizons, limens, thresholds, checkpoint stays,
whose gates turned back the merely curious
who lacked authority to scan the ways
    that open out past matter's spurious
containment of the facts that truly tell
the tale of spirit's play in furious
    descent down broken slopes, whose rapids well
below each breath, beneath each lucent eye.
The cosmos we behold's a stricken bell,
    rung for rousing, sounded to belie
somnambulism's all-embracing gull.
In truth we crawl, ant-wise, beneath a sky

   that maps the underside of our own skull.
We stray in sleep, imagine we awake
and walk through chambers walled by matter's lull,
   a labyrinthine palace, gothic brake,
whose involutions caught us in our fall:
home and dungeon, pillow, pyre and stake.
   With sceptre, crown of clutching thorns as pall,
we stoop, disgraced, by circumstances pent,
whose mockery, in vinegar and gall,
   cannot efface the fact of our descent
(however blocked our backward-bending gaze)
from shapes of former selves we underwent
   in other ages, light of elder days
that shade our present like a dative case
inherited from language's young ways.
   Once we could read the past like ancient lace,
translucent threads whose intersections meet
to form a scroll of more than history's trace,
   whose near end flapped and lapped at our own feet,
on sand where all's now foam and speechless waves,
which fascinate but cannot text or tweet.
   But if we still our minds before their caves,
and peer across the shingle, wrack, and sedge,
if ears attend the melancholy staves
   of winds that whistle from the sky's far edge,
we will recover something, grasp some haft
whose shovel-blade might show us how to dredge
   deep channels choked with silt, whose shallow draft
now bars all outlet to profounder deeps,
where we might steer our creaking, leaking craft,
   crewed by no more than phantoms in our sleeps,
towards such havens as we only dream,
while time in its slow revolutions creeps.

PANDEMICAL ASSAYS
in viro veritas

i. Into the Woods

Language leaps from ploughman's soil to sky,
forms words that wheel in flocks that murmurate
on errant winds. Semantic phantoms fly,
aeolian, fractal. Billows adumbrate
the figural beneath their folds. They swirl
this way and that on hermeneutic gusts.
The vortices of meaning rasp, unfurl,
and gather in piles, the legacy of lusts
that veer and stoop on thought like hawks that wind
the upper airs, invisible, rough powers
surveying all the corridors of mind
that we ourselves neglect, urged on by hours,
   pursuing chains of gaunt, delusive goods
     that draw us ever deeper through these woods.

ii. The Rock Ensouled

The spirits press upon us all around,
our unresponsive hearts dilapidate
like ruined chapels, consecrated ground,
thrown open towards the elements' dilate.
The offerings we laid upon the altar
no longer kindle; heaven's fires forebear
to lick the stones whose squared enjambments falter:

their upward ligaments grow taut and tear,
and from the air microbials descend
to mind us of past infelicities
that taught us to ignore the higher bend
of matter's telling eccentricities.
   The rock, lent careful ear, will spill its soul.
   Till then, not it nor we adventure whole.

iii. Going Viral

An *out*side without *in*, a spiky ball,
genomic embassy whose truths unscroll
from matter's clack and clatter down the hall
of space and time. No spirit stirs, no soul
to make a neighbour of the poorest bug.
Bitterly estranged from our arrears,
we gape all round us, groping through the fug
of unfamiliarity that smears
all scenes, leaves surfaces opaque,
like lungs that can't sort oxygen from air
and fail our pulmonary give and take,
communion of the self and world out there.
   As if some coup has interposed its mass,
   and wary sentries hold each mountain pass.

iv. The Ascent

And these are but the foothills, daunting ken,
rocky and perverse, mere leaning slopes

against the sky that rise but one in ten.
Not easy, but no bar to our far hopes.
Beyond though, in the middle distance, leap
the bluffs and sharp ascents that we must tame,
refusing to be daunted by their steep
forbidding brows that frown on us as lame
importunates, presuming thus to press
our right to those high prospects, whence we fell
through unremembered lives down from that ness,
exiles in the pits of being's well.
   Celestial promontory, rock and reef
     on which we founder upward through our grief.

v. *Apocalypsis*

The remembrancers that I let drop are veils.
Concealing to reveal, they bear my name,
curt monogrammed epitomes of tales
too long for book or chronicle to tame.
You lift them to your face: I am not there.
Your hands and eyes and nose alike deceive,
yet still my shadow lingers on the air,
fragrant like the threads of smoke that weave
a plume from fires somewhere down below,
whose fury none will feel until too late,
as towers lean, as Bedlam's warders throw
their keys away, and desolation's gate
   groans open slowly on a waking world
     where none dare see the banners thus unfurled.

vi. The Pneumatic Seismometer

Time washes down the slopes of living forms,
erodes the body's flesh declivities
in cataracts dispatched by distant storms
that growl in sullen inarticulacy
above, behind, upon the distant peaks
whence soul's descent began the whole beguine,
in rippled earth pitched forth on waves to seek
the outermost frontier of matter's scene.
The echoes ring, first light to final dark,
when all geography implodes to naught,
its ghost a hovering presence left to mark
the shapes of restless burgeon matter caught:
    seismometer of spirit's ruck and swell,
    unscrolling flicker of the needle's tell.

Requiescat

They crash in rolling waves upon the shore:
futilities of circumstance and chance
that never yield to any voiced implore
but gouge this coast with unrelenting dance

that forms a bay, a haven in whose lee
strange ships from far-off lands can furl their sails
and let the wind go whistle through the trees
whose roots clutch earth and crowns sweep starry trails.

From ocean's thrash to harbour's warding hand,
tossed prows that made no head against the churn
heave round to bury keels into the sand
beneath the silent moon, where watch-fires burn.

The March Lands

Perhaps he's strayed too long across this ground,
dry river beds and forests without leaf,
his inward scenes and outer swapped around,
subject to illusion, touched by grief,
pursuing tracks he fears might be his own,
circling round some secret *temenos*,
whose cryptic *influenza* sweeps a zone,
centripetal remembrancer of rose:
a maze, invisible, yet edged with thorn
that steers him by the sendings of his skin
from over the march he crossed when he was born,
whose no-man's land at last begins to thin.
   He sees the exit signs that spell out DEATH
   in Babel's tongues and draws another breath.

Selfie de l'Isle

Isle is just contraction of *I will,*
each atoll cradling no sure place at all,
a palm-fringed vacancy, creation's sill,
a frame and sash that pierce the nearest wall.
Laguna as *lacuna* in the text:
God's formative subjunctives held at bay,
a breathing space swept clear for what comes next,
a world whirled into shape like potter's clay,
an empty core lent form by coral ring,
its gloaming twined about by day and night,
whose alternate antiphony will sting
new life beneath the waters of the bight.
    Thus sun and self in mutual regard
      dance round the moon in tripping galliard.

www.ingramcontent.com/pod-product-compliance
Lightning Source LLC
Chambersburg PA
CBHW071404160426
42813CB00084B/463